AT SUMMER'S WISTFUL END

LAST POEMS FOR HALLOWEEN

Praise for *At Summer's Wistful End: Last Poems for Halloween*

"Half alchemist, half hypnotist, Opperman distills the quintessence of Halloween into rhythmic rhyming incantations; read them aloud to taste the candy corn, scent the cinnamon and cloves, and glimpse the eerie orange flame dancing in the jack-o'-lantern's gap-toothed grin. Samhain, Hop-tu-Naa, Ealra Hálgena Ǽfen... call it what you will: this book will make you yearn for the childlike euphoria that only happens on All Hallows' Eve."

— **Adam Bolivar**, author of *A Wheel of Ravens*
and *Ballads for the Witching Hour*

"K. A. Opperman acts as consummate seer to the witching season... each verse gleams like a mournful ember at the heart of a dying Samhain bonfire... This is poetry by one who has tread the Jack-o'-Lantern Path devoutly, ruminations and revelations from the heart of a dark reverence. Recommended for all souls who feel the draw of autumnal nights, who shiver in expectation as well as fear at the nearness of veil's parting."

— **Scott J. Couturier**, author of *I Awaken In October: Poems of Folk Horror and Halloween* and *The Box*

"Like one of his beloved jack-o'-lanterns, K. A. Opperman has carved a niche for himself as the doyen of Halloween-themed poetry... he gathers here the remaining poems in his bag of treats to offer up a final tribute to his favorite holiday. Opperman's love for everything from the changing colors of foliage to picking apples and the growing of pumpkins is represented. I have high hopes that this series will help spark a tradition of Halloween poetry to rival the abundance of carols, stories and poems for the Christmastide."

— **Manuel Arenas**, author of *Book of Shadows*
and *The Burning Ember Mission of Helldorado*

Praise for *October Ghosts and Autumn Dreams: More Poems for Halloween*

"K. A. Opperman's second book of Halloween poetry isn't just a celebration of that most beloved of dark festivals—it's a hypnotic dream weaver that cocoons the unwary (but fortunate) reader in a rich autumnal spell made up of pumpkins, the risen dead, and Halloween's special enchantment. This is a book to pick up anytime in the year when you need a dose of magic."

— **Lisa Morton**, author of
Trick or Treat: A History of Halloween

"*October Ghosts & Autumn Dreams* is an enchanting dive into all the beauty that encapsulates the autumnal spirit. From catchy rhythms to recite while carving jack-o-lanterns in 'Carver's Rhyme' to a well-researched look into Appalachian customs... every line is beautifully crafted and sure to be appreciated by anyone who is a fan of the spooky season!"

— **Heather Moser**, Producer of *Small Town Monsters*

"K. A. Opperman captures the bittersweet joy of Halloween and the sadness of its passing. Here are poems of childhood and poems of its loss... *October Ghosts* is Opperman the most at home, spooky, haunted and candle-lit though that home may be. Here is the poet's joy, laid bare and generously shared for readers young and old alike."

— **S. L. Edwards**, author of
Whiskey and Other Unusual Ghosts

Opperman's poems paint vivid pictures of autumn nights filled with nocturnal wonder. This collection is a heartfelt love letter to the season of dead leaves and glaring jack-o'-lanterns that imbues the reader with magical feelings of Halloweens past."

— **Curtis M. Lawson**, author of *Devil's Night*

Praise for *Past the Glad and Sunlit Season: Poems for Halloween*

"...[K. A. Opperman] is the gifted descendant of poets ranging from Poe to Walter Scott to Robert Burns, all of whom understood that Halloween's deliciously dark mood may be best served by poetry."

— From the Preface by **Lisa Morton**, author of
Trick or Treat: A History of Halloween

"K. A. Opperman's poems evoke both the dark chill of late October and the warmth of a cottage fireside. He captures a time outside of time, an otherworld populated by Pumpkin Kings and haunted souls who wander the edges of our consciousness begging to come inside. The book is a heartfelt incantation to mysteries of Halloween."

— **Lesley Pratt Bannatyne**, author of *Halloween:
An American Holiday, an American History*

"Halloweens past have often been preserved through verse and this collection brings that tradition forward, linking the heritage of old customs with the present and beyond. In the tradition of Burns or Poe, K. A. Opperman's *Past the Glad and Sunlit Season: Poems for Halloween* captures the spirit of the shadow and stirs up deep memories and hidden secrets of this time of the year. These visions of All Hallows' Eve are sure to enchant and whisk the reader away to a world of crisp autumn leaves, brimming with magic. The poems within this collection are steeped in folklore and perfectly reflect the ambiance of Halloween. This book will become your treasured new Halloween tradition."

— **Mickie Mueller**, author of *Llewellyn's
Little Book of Halloween*

Praise for *Past the Glad and Sunlit Season: Poems for Halloween*

"K. A. Opperman has gifted us a varied gathering of lovely, intelligent poems that swell from a passion for the magical black and orange season. Beautiful and evocative, the works are rich in imagery and mood, composed of intriguing rhyme schemes and word choices. Reading this collection made me think of the noble poetry of old, and the subject could not appeal to me more. *Past the Glad and Sunlit Season* is a treasure from a superb wordsmith whose love for the great season burns brighter than a thousand jack-o'-lanterns. I hereby dub Mr. Opperman the poet laureate of Halloween."

— **Scott Thomas**, author of *The Sea of Ash*

"Follow the flickering orange light into the darkness beyond Summer's End, and pay court to the Pumpkin King. . . . K. A. Opperman's passion for Halloween burns as brightly as Jack's fabled lantern. That, combined with his uncanny metrical precision, is a potent recipe for verse-magick that is as haunting as it is darkly delightful."

— **Adam Bolivar**, author of *The Lay of Old Hex*

"*Past the Glad and Sunlit Season* is a cornucopia of autumnal delights. At turns whimsical and sombre, K. A. Opperman's Halloween poems serve as fine evocations of that season of mist, fire, and scythe."

— **Richard Gavin**, author of *Sylvan Dread: Tales of Pastoral Darkness*

"All hail the Pumpkin King, aka K. A. Opperman! Those of us who love Halloween in all its guises will be delighted by this collection of seasonal poetry."

— **Denise Dumars**, author of *The Dark Archetype: Exploring the Shadow Side of the Divine*

Also by K. A. Opperman

The Crimson Tome

The Laughter of Ghouls

Past the Glad and Sunlit Season:
Poems for Halloween

October Ghosts and Autumn Dreams:
More Poems for Halloween

AT SUMMER'S WISTFUL END

LAST POEMS FOR HALLOWEEN

K. A. OPPERMAN

WITH ILLUSTRATIONS BY
DAN SAUER

JACKANAPES
PRESS

"Bard of Grain and Gourd" first appeared in *Spectral Realms* No. 18 (Hippocampus Press, Winter 2023)

"The Halloween Owl" first appeared in *Weird Fiction Quarterly* (Alien Sun Press, Fall 2023)

"Lords of Halloween" first appeared in *Penumbra* No. 4 (Hippocampus Press, Fall 2023)

"Loweena the Witch" first appeared in *Weird Fiction Quarterly* (Alien Sun Press, Fall 2023)

"My October Bride" first appeared in *Weird Fiction Quarterly: Folk Horror* (Alien Sun Press, Spring 2024)

"October is Coming" first appeared in *Spectral Realms* No. 15 (Hippocampus Press, Summer 2021)

"October's Fruit" first appeared in *Eternal Haunted Summer* (Summer 2024)

"Pumpkin Ale" first appeared in *Spectral Realms* No. 18 (Hippocampus Press, Winter 2023)

All other poems collected herein are original to this publication.

First Paperback Edition
1 3 5 7 9 8 6 4 2

ISBN: 978-1-956702-14-9

For Ashley,
my October Bride

CONTENTS

I. OCTOBER PROPHECIES

II. AUTUMN GLOAMING

III. QUIET ALTARS

APPENDICES

ILLUSTRATIONS

INTRODUCTION

SEASON
OF
WHISPERS

These words form the beginning of a book, and yet they are also an ending—for here follows the final volume in a trilogy, the last entry in the Poems for Halloween series. It may be that this constitutes the end of the road for my singing of songs about the black and orange season; or, it may not. What is certain is that a chapter now comes to a close, and what new chapters may or may not await down the twilit autumn road of life, just around the hay-baled bend, I cannot yet tell.

Past the Glad and Sunlit Season, with its gleefully garish pumpkin-orange cover—the breakout first volume in the Poems for Halloween series—remains the most popular book I have ever written. *October Ghosts and Autumn Dreams*, the second volume in the series, is in my estimation a very solid followup, more of the exact same kind of autumnal charms. This third and final volume, *At Summer's Wistful End*, I can only hope, will prove a fitting and triumphant end to the series, like the last fanfare of a vintage cardboard bugle blown on Halloween night, perhaps accompanied by the crazy jangle of a tambourine, and the raucous cacophony of tin shakers and clickers.

There have been some significant changes in my life between the completion of the previous book and the writing of this third volume, and with these new chapters have also come new Halloween experiences to nourish my poetic imagination, like rich, black soil beneath autumn mushrooms. Despite this, as I close the cover on this third and final book, inspiration has begun to wane. The flame burns but dimly... goblin-blue, smoldering in shadow, entombed inside a moist, half-rotten gourd—yet never quite ready to expire. For now at least, I feel I've said almost all I have to say about Samhain and its Season of Whispers; therefore, this book shall indeed mark a chapter's close.

But dead leaves rarely lie still for long—in October.

* * *

Whether or not I—or anyone else, for that matter—continue to tell the grand and benighted tales of autumns lost to time, Halloween will, of course, forever live on. I don't think, though, that we'll ever find ourselves without a troupe of October Bards to sing us the Black and Orange Songs, the Hallowed Hymns, the Pumpkin Paeans. The ancient whispers of Halloween demand to be heard, bleeding blackly through quills by candlelight, and sighing in the barren October boughs. It is the silent voice that talks through the crooked grins of jack-o'-lanterns; the cunning, devious voice that speaks through a child's chanting of trick-or-treat. Such a voice cannot be suppressed, and there will always be those of us who listen carefully, and channel it willingly.

I heard this voice as I walked through my apartment complex last Halloween, looking for signs of the holiday's persistence in this strange new environment so far removed from the neighborhood of my childhood home. Sadly, the heart of Halloween does not beat as persistently in every place of residence—but I was overjoyed to find that the holiday thrived in this new environment. A pair of children, dressed in vintage-looking costumes of skeleton and devil, darted through lamplight and shadows shouting those three time-honored words, "trick-or-treat!" Parents trailed their young goblins, reveling in this masquerade-night of mischief and mystery. Macabre decorations and orange and purple lights garlanded door-steps, hedges, and fences. Jack-o'-lanterns cast their fey, darkling light over dewy, leaf-strown lawns and slate-gray sidewalks. Even a black cat or two came skulking through the scene, curious about the human proceedings unfolding on this brisk autumnal night. In short—

It was a perfect Halloween.

In many ways, I have come full-circle. I have now welcomed trick-or-treaters to my very own doorstep, and I have lit my very own jack-o'-lantern blow-mold upon my balcony, delighting children even as I myself was once mesmerized by the glowing plastic pumpkin on a neighbor's fence. I have strung up scarecrow, witch, and ghost, and I have garlanded the eaves with artificial foliage of gold and crimson. Above all, I have kept the authentic gourd-carven jack-o'-lantern dutifully lit upon my October porch, even as his brethren begin to give way to electric simulacra.

This book brings us full-circle, too. Truly, we come to Summer's End. But in that ending, we find the shadowy door of memory, leading back to the beginning. To childhood. To dim corridors lost to time. We walk them now—as echoes. As ghosts. As strangers in our own forgotten lives.

All three of these collections have poured forth from the cauldron of my memories with the deepest sincerity. I have sought to celebrate and preserve my most precious experiences, sensations, and impressions from Halloweens of yore, while also endeavoring to document the ever-evolving traditions of that fabled day; those that abide as of old, and those newly emergent. I have done the very best I know how to do, carving my words as a child carves their jack-o'-lantern: true of heart, and steady of hand. I set these new poems out on the darkened porch for you now.

May they shine, with faces grim and gleeful.

—K. A. Opperman
Rowland Heights, California
16 April 2024

I

OCTOBER
PROPHECIES

The Pumpkin Path

So hidden is the pumpkin path
That few the way can follow—
One needs to trust the ancient faith,
The candle in the hollow.

A pumpkin here, a pumpkin there,
And sometimes not in season—
They really could be anywhere,
Without a seeming reason.

But those of us who know the way,
We recognize the beacons—
The signal-fires of the fay,
The hidden road that beckons.

So hidden is the pumpkin path
That few will ever find it—
Except perhaps a wayward wraith,
Or the goblins that designed it.

October's Fruit

Like two green fingers reaching from the grave—
Claws of a witch who comes to wreak her curse—
The pumpkin sprout emerges from a cave
Of loam and mulch its creepers to disperse.

It is the first to rise, a wilding seed
That overwintered 'neath the leaves and moss—
Even in spring October's fruit must breed;
Even in summer ripens autumn's loss.

September Comes Too Quickly

September comes too quickly,
October soon is gone;
The maple, sparse and sickly,
In crimson shrouds the lawn.

The last remaining acorn
Drops tear-like from the oak,
While Luna, white and bicorn,
Ascends as ravens croak.

Mabon

Strange gourds are on the mantle,
Fall flowers wreathe the door;
Old treasures sentimental
Now haunt my house once more.

The scent of spice and apple
Hangs ghost-like in the air,
While candle-shadows dapple
Dim walls my dreams to snare.

Humble Harvest

This is my humble harvest,
Two pumpkins of a pair—
One each to keep and carve, lest
My hearth and porch go bare.

But though my yields be humble,
No farmer's golden share,
The yellow bees that bumble
Have wealth enough to spare.

Chant of Protection

Spirit and spider, goblin and bat,
Black cat and witch with a tall pointy hat,
Skeleton, screech-owl, toad or a rat—
Pumpkin, let none past my welcoming mat!

Bard of Grain and Gourd

For Scott J. Couturier

He sings us pumpkin paeans, spectral chants
That prophecy October's chill return.
With druid concentration, he incants
Autumnal spells to help the bonfires burn.

A bard of amber grain and ruddied gourd—
Of grapes that purple on September vines—
His wistful dreams are turned forever toward
October's golden gate, which dimly shines.

October is Coming

October is coming, as sure as the scythe
Will sweep through the fields of grain.
October is coming, though summer is blithe—
It's just round the bend in the lane.

October is coming, as pumpkins foretell,
Appearing in markets and farms.
October is coming, its mystical spell
Is changing the world with its charms.

October is coming, with cinnamon spice—
With pie and with cider and cake.
October is coming, with treats to entice
Lost children from dreaming to wake.

October is coming, so say your goodbyes
To youth and to yesterday's glow.
The crows are a-circling on violet skies,
And leaves toward oblivion blow.

Pumpkin Spice

Cinnamon, ginger, nutmeg, clove
Are the spices that I love.
Put them in a pumpkin pie—
Or anything else you'd like to try.

Cinnamon, ginger, nutmeg, clove
Wafting from the kitchen stove,
Steaming from my cup of tea—
O pumpkin spice is the spice for me!

Pumpkin Ale

An orange potion steeped with pumpkin spice,
Recalling autumns lost, and yet to be,
This rustic ale casts such witchery
Over my soul, my fancy to entice.

This is the kiss of witches candy-sweet,
Like cinnamon on apple-shapen lips....
Beneath a spell, with ever deeper sips,
I grow unsteady on my hay-strown seat.

Now all the owls sing a goblin song,
And bats foretell October's chill approach;
Such haunting strains of cricket-chirps encroach
On twilight silence—it will not be long.

It won't be long till autumn hangs her flags
Of gold and crimson in the sighing trees,
And so I drain my flagon to the lees,
And dream of scarecrows, kings in tattered rags.

October First

An orange X has marked the blank white square
Whereon is writ in black October 1st—
The calendar dissolves upon the air,
Revealing scenes idyllic and accursed.

A thousand grins, grotesque and glad alike,
All smile and mock me—pumpkin, ghost, and witch;
In hearts of all who pass, their gazes strike
Both fun and fear, from porch and window-niche.

Both fun and fear...the roots of trick-or-treat
Are intertwined within this twilight scene,
Where children scamper down a lamp-lit street
To hasten home ere come of Halloween.

But as their doors creak shut on autumn dark,
Against a gust of hissing, crimson leaves—
I look once more upon a crooked mark
Drawn in a box, and dream of coming eves.

II

AUTUMN
GLOAMING

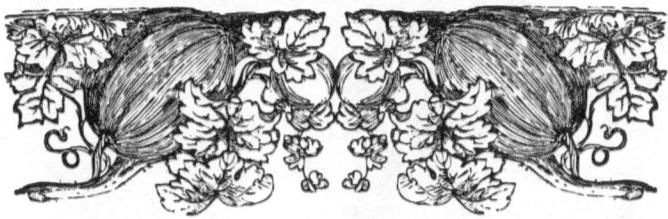

Pumpkin Creek

Pumpkin Creek
Is a sleepy town
Where mill-wheels creak,
And leaves fall down,
Plum and gold,
Red and brown,
Gems to deck October's gown.

Pumpkin Creek
Is a peaceful place
Where barns antique
Still bear the trace
Of ways of old—
Their hex-signs grace
The gateside gourds in lieu of a face.

Pumpkin Creek
Is far, yet near—
A place you seek
Near the end of the year,
When nights grow cold,
And days grow drear,
And Halloween is almost here.

October Idyll

October is time
To brazenly climb
A haystack and take in the view
Of harvested farms,
Where everyone's arms
Are full with a pumpkin or two.

October's blue skies,
So soft on the eyes,
Invite you to lie on the grass
And languidly gaze,
On strange golden days,
At clouds that phantasmally pass.

Devil's Night

It's Devil's Night, it's Devil's Night,
The night of mischief, fiends, and fright,
When bonfires cast their crimson light
On pitchfork, mask, and cloak.

It's Devil's Night, it's Devil's Night,
When pranks are played in ancient rite—
When gutted gourds are blazing bright,
And laugh among the smoke.

It's Devil's Night, it's Devil's Night,
When ravens flee in sunset flight,
And briefly form a haunting sight—
A devil newly woke.

It's Devil's Night, it's Devil's Night,
So shut your windows, latch them tight;
October's masque will reach its height
At midnight's wicked stroke.

Oíche Shamhna

Oíche Shamhna, night of spirits,
Eve of Samhain, summer's end,
When the Shadow is so near its
World with ours begins to blend.

Oíche Shamhna, light the fires,
Cast the bones into the blaze;
Drive the livestock past the pyres,
Purified for darker days.

Oíche Shamhna, set the table—
leave it vacant for the dead;
Honor them if you are able,
Leave them apples, beer and bread.

Oíche Shamhna, sidhe are roaming—
Earn their favor with a treat.
Turnips grin in autumn gloaming,
Till the harvest is complete.

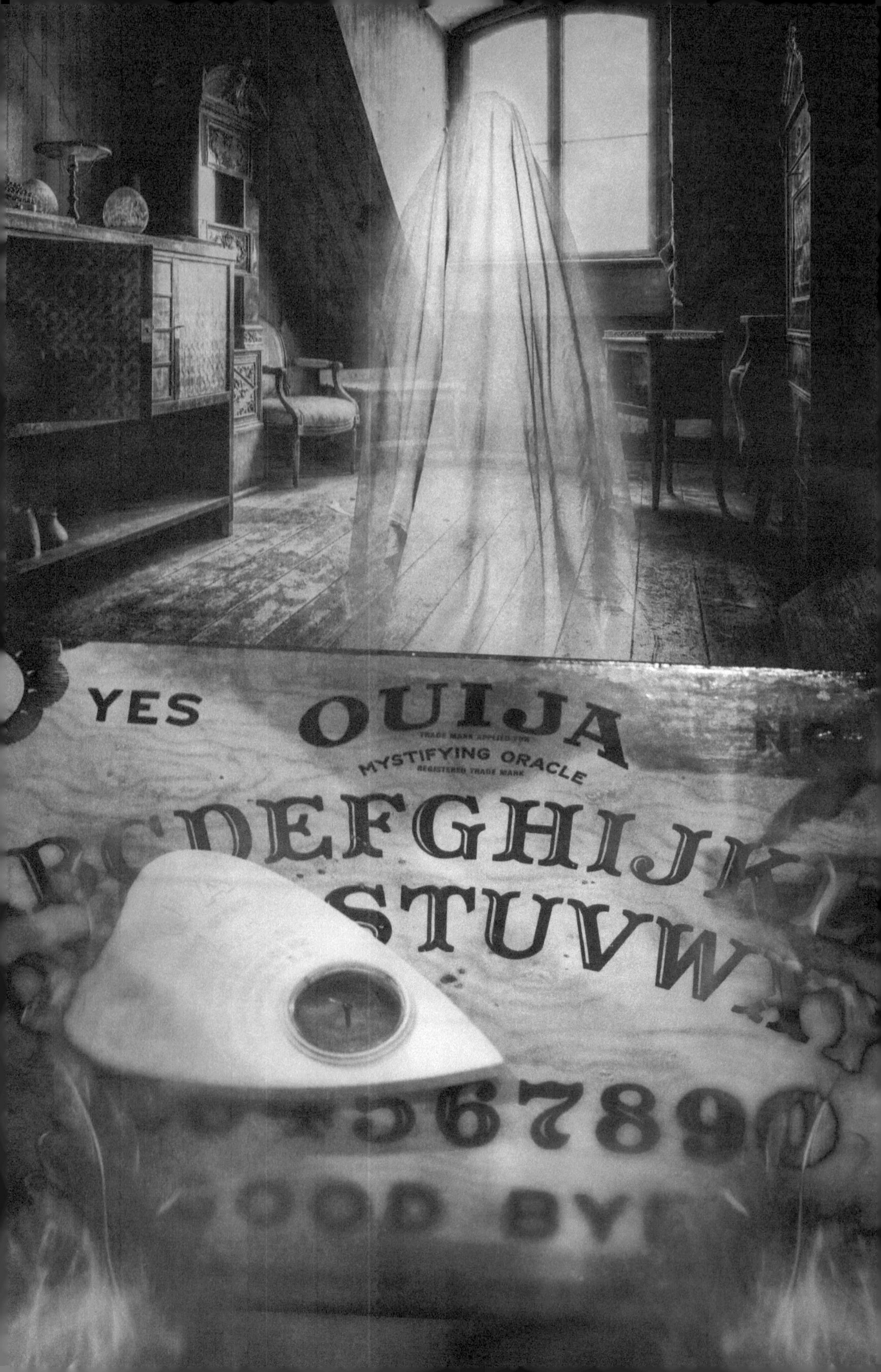
YES
OUIJA
MYSTIFYING ORACLE
DEFGHIJ
STUVW
67890

Ouija Board

A B C D E F G,
Ouija board, I conjure thee:
Tell us what your mystic Eye
From out the spirit world can spy.

1 2 3 4 5 6 7,
Spirits come from hell or heaven;
Push the planchette round the board
Until it spells for us a word.

YES or NO, NO or YES,
Play this spectral game of chess:
Place your fingertips so gently,
Focus on the flame intently....

Sun and Moon, Moon and Star,
By the witching powers that are,
Guide for us the mystic Eye,
Until it's time to say GOODBYE.

The Halloween Horn

When I sound my Halloween horn
The spooks and spirits all are sworn
To answer its resounding call,
No matter it be in summer or fall.

When I sound my Halloween horn,
This cardboard bugle old and torn,
The faded ghosts of olden days
All dance by jack-o'-lanterns' blaze.

The King of October

O what is that light on a dark autumn night,
O what is that welcoming glow?
O what is the name of that flickering flame?—
Please tell me, I'd sure like to know.

My name it is Jack-o'-th'-Lantern, I lack
No fame, I am known all around.
From pumpkin I'm made, with a spoon and a blade,
And King of October I'm crowned.

No Pumpkins

This poem has no pumpkins,
No jack-o'-lantern grins,
No patches full of pumpkins,
No porch with orange twins.

This poem has no pumpkins,
No autumn squash in sight—
But when it comes to pumpkins,
I think they're quite alright!

Pumpkin Apotheosis

I am more gourd than man, orange syrup runs
Throughout my veins and spreads vermilion vines.
Inside my soul, a darkling lantern shines—
I have become one of the Hallowed Ones.

Lords of Halloween

Though we sleep and though we slumber,
Buried in November graves,
We will rise in greater number
When again the cornstalk waves.

Though our masks and costumes crumple—
Pumpkin, burlap, purple leaves—
We will be the ones to trample
Down the furrows and the sheaves.

We will come like living torches,
We will come with smiles of flame;
Set a pumpkin on your porches,
Lest we come your souls to claim.

We will come with scythe and sickle
Glinting with a moonlit sheen;
We are fate, and fate is fickle—
We are lords of Halloween.

Grin

That certain flicker of a candle-flame
Flashing like lightning from a pumpkin's face—
No other thing affects me in the same
Bewitching way, dispelling time and space.

That certain savor of a pumpkin's flesh
As it is slowly roasted from within—
With every whiff my memories are fresh,
And like my lantern, once again—I grin.

The Stain

A pumpkin rotted on my hearth
One Halloween agone—
It tried returning to the earth,
But found no autumn lawn.

It only found unyielding stone,
And left there but a stain,
Within whose murk has slowly grown
The grimace of the slain.

The Candy Chute

All wrapped around with orange and purple lights,
The candy chute delivers sweet delights
Down into pillowcase and candy-pail—
All Hallows' Eve will evermore prevail.

With pinwheel stripes that spiral down, down, down,
Like something painted by a circus clown,
The chute emerges through a lurking grin,
The ghost of plague, and will not let it win.

The Halloween Owl

There is an owl that hoots on Halloween,
For one night only, and no other night.
With magic plumage yellow, orange, and green,
The creature makes a most majestic sight.

It is good luck to spot this goblin bird,
But in exchange it likes a tiny gift—
Of what you see you cannot say a word,
To any questions you must give short shrift....

The owl will swoop to take a single piece
Of colored candy while you trick-or-treat,
And in its haunting song it will not cease
Until its candy harvest is complete.

Then to its festive nest it will return,
Clutching a pumpkin-bucket full of spoils,
To hibernate while seasons take their turn,
Amid the sparkling wrappers, golden foils.

The Black Cat

The black cat slinks when an orange moon winks
And the spooks come out to play.
You will hear him yowl when the great horned owl
Takes wing at the end of day.

See him arch his back on the country track
With a flash of his emerald eyes!
Hear his wicked hiss as you narrowly miss
Stepping on him by surprise.

Bad luck, thirteen, it's Halloween—
You fear the black cat's curse!
But you need not fear, though the night is drear—
Your fate could be far worse.

He's not bad luck, no goblin or puck,
But an omen and a sign
That the witch who lives in the woodland gives
You her blessing nine times nine.

In the Circle of Seven Jack-o'-Lanterns

Encircled round by seven jack-o'-lanterns,
I drink the witch-wine, chanting to the heavens.
This is the night of goblins, gnomes, nicnevins;
What wicked grins from shadows black, O lanterns!

Which way I glance, a glowing face regards me,
Like pumpkin pookas that would have me wander
Into the devil-haunted darkness yonder—
And yet against such ghosts the circle guards me.

A witch's broom is leaning near beside me,
And everywhere the Veil is growing thinner;
In autumn magic I am no beginner—
And yet a hint of terror stirs inside me.

Encircled round by seven jack-o'-lanterns,
I drink the witch-wine, chanting to the heavens—
And spy a monstrous cat-face fanged with levins—
The magic circle must not crack, O lanterns—!

Autumn Witch

Her jack-o'-lantern cauldron smiles
As emerald slime is swirled within;
The red-haired witch, with all her wiles,
Prepares her brew while baring skin.

She summons fools to try her treats—
Some apples, or perhaps some pie?
She dishes up her wicked sweets—
But bones and toadstools do not lie....

Too late they heed the telltale signs—
Too late they hear the viper's hiss.
What first appeared as pumpkin vines,
Her pet now earns the witch's kiss.

Encoiled around her pointed hat,
The serpent watches as they fall,
So soon entombed beneath a mat
Of autumn leaves, and moonlight's pall.

—After the artwork "Autumn Witch," by Rebecca Whitaker

Loweena the Witch

With swirling hair of autumn flame,
And feline eyes of emerald green,
Loweena was the witch's name—
Loweena Halloween.

A nightshade shadow lined her eyes,
Her lips an apple red and ripe;
She soared upon October skies,
With imps of every stripe.

And all who saw Loweena soar
Against the haunting, orange moon
Saw something they could not ignore,
Which made them all to swoon:

Upon her curvy derriere,
Beneath her wind-uplifted hem,
A coal-black pumpkin face did stare
So darkly down at them.

The Scarecrow Maiden

A scarecrow maiden made of straw
Watched over farm and field;
No matter how the crows would caw,
Her crops she would not yield.

Starched burlap formed her pretty face,
Her lashes, sewn-on seeds;
Her dress and crown were made of lace,
And feathers, flowers and weeds.

October witchcraft gave her life,
A presence often felt;
And whether in times of wealth or strife,
To her, the farmers knelt.

They paid their worship one and all,
Begged bounty over dearth—
None but the sunflower stood as tall
As the doll of Mother Earth.

My October Bride

White pumpkins lined the woodland aisle,
Dim lanterns lent their light;
The arch was wreathed in sylvan style
With violets, tulle of white;
The faeries sang a haunting tune,
A raven darkly cried;
Through sunset branches beamed the moon
For my October Bride.

Behind her trailed a night-black veil,
Her dress was emerald-green;
She walked upon an autumn trail
So near to Halloween.
The members of her retinue
Wore horn and mask and hide;
The Forest Host the ox-horn blew
For my October Bride.

She drifted down the bridal lane,
A goddess ghostly fair;
An onyx crown adorned her mane
Of lustrous raven hair;
Her eyes they were the twilight blue
Of welkins dusky-skied;
My love was pure, my love was true
For my October Bride.

We gathered for the ancient rite
Of marriage, joining hands;
A silken cord secured them tight,
The style of Celtic lands.
So cold, though, were her fingertips
I thought she sure had died;
I leant to kiss the purple lips
Of my October bride.

The twilight woods became a blur
Of russet, red, and gold;
Still fastened by the hand to her,
My soul at last was sold.
The Wild Hunt swept upon the mist
To take me for their Ride,
My steed beside the one I'd kissed,
My fair October Bride.

And now I dwell forevermore
Within her woodland hall,
Where silver cups forever pour,
And antlers crown the wall.
Amid a phantom masquerade,
I sit here by her side,
Forever bound by magic braid
To my October bride.

III

QUIET
ALTARS

Dead Leaves

Dead leaves are lying on the ground,
A patchwork quilt upon the grass;
The sidewalk crunches with their sound
As down the lane I slowly pass.

Such colors—scarlet, russet, plum—
Are present in their rich array,
That one can hardly still be glum
To see them on an autumn day.

But when the wind begins to blow,
Like ghostly hands that comb the trees—
When sadly calls a lonely crow—
I'm haunted by old memories.

Dead leaves remind me of what was,
And what shall never be again—
Time blows away, it always does,
Days lost like leaves in yonder glen.

Autumn Thoughts

My thoughts are as sere as the rotting red leaves
That wayward at twilight will blow;
My thoughts are the hiss of the shivering sheaves—
I know what the scarecrows all know.

My thoughts are the flicker of witch-light, the flame
Of pumpkins that laugh in the dark;
The slice of the scythe-blade that stakes a cruel claim—
The gleam of its merciless arc.

This Halloween

This Halloween
Will be the one—
The perfect scene
At set of sun;
My autumn dream
Come true at last...
As candles gleam
Sad light to cast.

This Halloween
Will be the end—
Though grass is green,
The bough must bend
To scatter leaves
Upon the grave—
This eve of eves
My heart will save.

Extinguished

Their flames gone out, their life has fled
Into the realm of memory.
Like skulls as frozen as the dead,
The gourds have lost all glamoury.

I say goodbye, they sadly grin
With gladness of a bygone day—
These pumpkins have become the kin
Of ghosts that slowly fade away.

Unhallowed Grave

The gourds at last are thrown away,
To come again another day,
And in their stead are left but seeds
And wax a jack-o'-lantern bleeds.

The porches now are barren, save
For Halloween's unhallowed grave,
But from the shade they shall return—
The lanterns there that once did burn.

Jack-o'-Lantern Curse

May your smile be carved with knives,
May your heart be hollow;
May you live the darkest of lives,
By only a witch's tallow.

The Jack-o'-Lantern's Mark

I've seen those souls who bear the mark—
The haunted stare, the mournful smile;
They wander through the autumn dark,
Through drifting leaves, for mile on mile.

Their light has almost guttered out,
And yet they serve as ghostly guide
To those in pain, in fear, and doubt,
At twilight's end, when light has died.

One Last Little Jack-o'-Lantern

One last little jack-o'-lantern,
Light my lonely way;
Martinmas has come and gone,
And the days are cold and gray.

One last little jack-o'-lantern
Carved in November's gloom,
Light my way to Yuletide's dawn
When the sun climbs from its tomb.

October Lament

Coldly blows the wind in October,
Coldly blows the sorrowful wind;
Seas of leaves that scrape on the pavement,
Seas of dreams that come to an end.

Coldly blows the wind in October,
Coldly fall the curtains of night;
Evening brings the ghost of bereavement—
Far, so far, the lamp's amber light.

Servant of the Olden Ways

My face is changeless like a carven gourd,
Emotionless, unmoving, cold and dead;
My gaze is strange, and turned forever toward
Far dreams of autumn where the leaves turn red.

I serve the olden ways of Halloween,
A skeleton, a scarecrow made of straw;
The coming darkness is my only queen—
The Wheel's turning is my only law.

The Throne of Gourd and Bone

No one can own a day like Halloween—
Except, perhaps, for phantoms in the mist.
No one can claim to be its king or queen,
Unless the rustling corn their name has hissed.

No one can claim the throne of gourd and bone
Unless they've passed beyond the twilight veil—
This night is given to the dead alone,
And only one forgotten shall we hail.

Black Laurels

It is my destiny to fade
Into the ashen mist of dusk,
To join the faeries in their rade,
A fallen leaf, a hollow husk.

Few mortal souls will mark my death,
And fewer still will shed a tear,
But on October's icy breath
Will blow my name for all to hear.

My name will flicker on the tongues
Of pumpkins in laments of flame,
The owls with their mournful songs
The choir of my eldritch fame.

I will be known unto the witch,
And all of her nocturnal kin—
In life, though neither loved, nor rich,
In death black laurels will I win.

Quiet Altars

It is enough to hang a paper ghost
Up in your window on that hallowed night,
And if it be the best that you can boast,
One jack-o'-lantern's grin is quite alright.

You need no riches, only straw-stuffed rags
To build a scarecrow to bewitch your lawn,
And all your lanterns, draped with paper bags
Cut out with skulls, can guide the dead till dawn.

The hallowed spirits heed no cheap display
Of store-bought goblins, bright-red blood and gore—
They pay their favor at the end of day
At quiet altars to the ways of yore.

Be ever faithful to the ancient ways,
And you will find the gold at summer's end—
The candy cauldron touched by sunset's rays,
Whose sugared coinage you will one day spend.

Candy Sorting

I pour my candy on the carpet floor,
That old brown carpet soft and worn with time;
I shake the bag, ensuring there's no more,
Then sort my candy, waiting midnight's chime.

The room is dim, the only pallid light
The television's otherworldly glow;
Skull, witch, and scarecrow, icons of the night,
Hang on the walls and watch my game below.

The long and winding trail of trick-or-treat
At last has ended, in my haunted home.
My autumn pilgrimage is now complete,
My wild adventure through October's gloom.

And now I sort this patchwork candy-pile,
Remembering each door along the way....
These Hallows' Even treats may last awhile—
But memories will never fade away.

At Summer's Wistful End

The evening slowly slips away
On wisps of curling smoke;
I mourn the last October day—
The spell has nearly broke.

The haunted clock has crept too near
To twelve—for I would spend
Another evening dreaming here
At summer's wistful end.

A treat or two is all that's left
Upon the porch's plate,
But lest the spirits go bereft,
I leave these treats to fate.

I shut the door upon the dark,
'Gainst gusts of leaves to fend,
While still the pumpkin bears a spark
To summer's wistful end.

The night becomes a memory,
As lost as are the dead—
But through some autumn gramarye,
The then and now are wed.

I bid goodbye to Halloween,
As to a dear old friend—
While faded laughter sings the threne
Of summer's wistful end.

APPENDICES

OCTOBER CHECKLIST

Several years ago, feeling unsure that I had made the most of the Halloween season, I made this checklist of activities that, where possible, I consider it necessary, or at least highly desirable, to partake of every October. Whenever I fear I may have strayed from the leaf-littered, candy-wrapped path that winds through October, I can turn to this list, which appears here almost verbatim as I first wrote it. Perhaps it may serve you as well.

* * *

- Shop for Halloween items and antiques in several stores, especially stores decorated for the season.

- Visit a pumpkin patch, pick a pumpkin there, and do other rustic or carnival activities there.

- Spend plenty of time outside, looking at decorations and, if possible, fall foliage.

- Carve and light a pumpkin, and also look at other lit jack-o'-lanterns.

- Harvest and carve a pumpkin you have grown yourself.

- Partake of many seasonal foods and beverages.

- Decorate for and properly observe the night of Halloween.

- Visit a haunted attraction, ghost tour, fall fair, or any other such seasonal event.

- Watch Halloween and/or horror movies.

- Write new Halloween poems, or create new Halloween artworks.

- Read new Halloween books, whether fiction or nonfiction.

- Engage with the liminal or otherworldly in some manner.

TRAVERSING THE VEIL

SOME IDEAS FOR EXPLORING THE LIMINAL IN OCTOBER

It is said that on the night of Halloween, the Veil between our world and the spirit world is at its thinnest. Therefore, in my opinion, any proper celebration of the October season ought to involve some sort of engagement with the liminal or otherwordly. I myself call this Traversing the Veil, and there are a number of ways that it can be done. What exactly this means, or how it can be done, is of course a subjective matter, as vague and insubstantial as the Veil itself, but here I will offer some of my own ideas on how to approach the Threshold— perchance, for a fleeting moment, to cross it.

Many of the activities commonly associated with the season already allow one to engage with the autumnally liminal to some degree. However, here are some additional ideas for those who wish to explore further what it means to Traverse the Veil.

- Take a nighttime stroll, opening yourself up to the full witchery of autumn.

- Visit a graveyard, the haunted ground between life and death.

- Visit a place known to be haunted.

- Meditate at night, near an open window, opening yourself up to whatever influences may waft in on the night-air.

- Use a divination device to learn your fortune.

- Maintain a seasonal altar, decorated appropriately.

- Leave out an offering, either for your ancestors, or for the spirits of the season, as a show of respect.

POEM NOTES

Here follow some potentially interesting tidbits regarding the back-stories of many of the poems in this book. As with the Poem Notes in the previous two volumes, not every poem has an entry: only those poems about which I definitely had something to say are represented here.

The Pumpkin Path

Like many of my poems, this one is inspired by true events. I recall going to the post office one day—a day very far removed from the Halloween season—and spotting a pumpkin seed lying on the grass outside of it. A little later, as I continued my errands, I espied a pumpkin on a desk at the bank. On another day, not too long after, while driving around exploring an interesting neighborhood, I spotted a house with two pumpkins on its stone gate-posts. To me, it seemed as if I was following some kind of hidden Pumpkin Path that no one could see or understand but me. These sorts of little signs signify to me that I am following the path aright—wherever it may lead.

October's Fruit

As an avid gardener, there have been many times when seeds planted during the previous season have sprouted unexpectedly in the next. They often emerge very early in the growing season, knowing exactly when the sunlight and temperature is just right for them. It is always a wondrous thing when such a sprout announces its presence. I unfailingly take it as an auspicious sign—yet it is poetic to contemplate how autumn's ruin has already taken root in the abundance of spring. It is all one continuum of growth and dissolution, of birth and death, cyclic and endless.

One-Hundred Days to Halloween

This is my true impression of the weather on this day last year. I distinctly remember the strange way in which the sun fought to penetrate the dreamy haze, and I remember a ghostly gust of wind nipping at my heels, and scattering brown, dead leaves, as I walked out of work for the day.

Tomorrow Comes September

I wrote this poem right on the heels of the previous poem—I think it may have been the very next day. I was still bewitched by the same pervading atmosphere, and as you can see, more words came of it. This would have been in late July, so it seems I didn't mean "tomorrow" in the literal sense. Though many of my poems are based on actual occurrences from my life, I am sometimes loose with the factual details, in order to suit my poetic aims.

September Comes Too Quickly

I used to compose a lot of my poems on my cell-phone, typing them into a notes file while on break at work. I'd think of the lines while working, and record them as soon as I could. This particular poem was nothing more than a note on my phone for I believe a year or two before I finally typed it into my computer. I never felt that it amounted to much, but ultimately I decided to preserve it for posterity, in case someone should find enjoyment in it. Ultimately, the poem conveys the sick feeling I sometimes experience when I contemplate how quickly my favorite season passes me by, every single year. All we can do is embrace the transience of it, the fey, fleeting magic that October brings.

Mabon

Mabon is a pagan holiday or festival celebrated late in September, on the Autumnal Equinox. It is also known as the Second Harvest (Lughnasadh being the First, and Samhain/Halloween being the last). This poem is so titled because I wrote it on the actual day of this holiday. By this time, almost anywhere you look, Halloween Season is in full swing—including at my house, while I was growing up. The "treasures sentimental" I mention in line 3 refer directly, among other seasonal heirlooms, to a ceramic haunted house owned by my mother. It is the one item I remember being displayed during the Halloweens of my childhood which she still places out to this day. It is a physical link to my most distant past—and therefore, it is priceless to me.

Humble Harvest

This poem is a true reference to a year when I was only able to grow two small pumpkins. I deemed that to be a suitable number—one for the porch, and one for the hearth; one inside, and one outside. I will also mention that I am quite fond of bees—I enjoy watching them grow fuzzy with golden pollen as they clamber in and out of my pumpkin flowers. They are nature's little helpers, ensuring pumpkins will get pollinated and grow to glorious size.

Bard of Grain and Gourd

This poem was written upon the publication of Scott J. Couturier's ebullient poetry collection, *I Awaken in October,* as both a commemoration and commendation. In my estimation, this author's uniquely reverent approach to the Halloween Season, and those long months of agricultural toil leading up to it, is the closest to my own that I have ever encountered in another individual. Our poetic voices and styles are a little different, but I believe we see and regard our shared subject matter in much the same way.

Pumpkin Spice

I love just about anything pumpkin spice flavored. Perhaps my favorite item of all is the famed Pumpkin Spice Latte, offered by the coffee chain Starbucks every fall for the last 20 years. Every year, in late August, I get one (iced) as soon as it becomes available.

Pumpkin Ale

Another one of my seasonal traditions is to partake of various pumpkin ales every Halloween season. Ideally I like to try at least one new one every year, but it becomes more and more difficult to come across pumpkin-bewitched brews I haven't tried yet. Luckily, pumpkin beer continues to increase in popularity, furthering the odds that I'll continue to discover new orange-tinted elixirs for years to come.

October First

The first day of October has always seemed to me to be just as freighted with witchery as Halloween itself. It is equally an ominous and mystical day—a day of portent and promise. You can feel a certain weight in the air, a gravity. The leaves fall so quietly and carefully, so as not to disturb or become enmeshed in the delicate web of the unseen that thickens like cobwebs over bush and branch, blanching the very air....

Pumpkin Creek

This poem wholly arose out of the mere name itself—Pumpkin Creek. The name was suggested to me by a friend, and this poem was simply my imagining of what such a place might be like.

October Idyll

I must admit that this poem was intended to be longer, but that I lost focus and abandoned it. It is essentially a fragment, but I felt that it stood on its own well enough to be included in this collection.

Devil's Night

For those who may not know, Devil's Night is October 30th, the night before Halloween. Traditionally, it is a night associated with mischief and destruction, and is grimly associated with the malevolent setting of fires.

Oíche Shamhna

Oíche Shamhna—I'll refrain from even attempting to explain the pronunciation—is the old Irish way of saying Halloween, or "Samhain Eve." In this poem, I attempted to illustrate Halloween in the very old and historical sense.

The Halloween Horn

This poem was inspired by an actual cardboard horn I found in a warehouse at my work. This warehouse offered old merchandise and various other items for sale at discount to employees, and quite by chance, I happened upon the old-looking Halloween horn for, I think, one dollar. Such items were sometimes used for seasonal décor, and I figured it must be one such item—surely a cheap reproduction. As fate would have it, though, research conducted later revealed it to be an authentic vintage Halloween item. Yes, I did blow the horn, ancient though it was...it seemed somehow appropriate to send forth one last obnoxious, blaring note to resurrect the days of yore.... Who knows how long it had been since that horn last sang its celebratory, autumnal tune.

No Pumpkins

My friends and acquaintances like to tease me, saying I only write poems about pumpkins. While this is not entirely inaccurate... I did feel the need to write this humorous little poem in response.

Lords of Halloween

This title or epithet was first used by a friend of mine, to describe both himself and me, and, much as in the case with the title "Pumpkin Creek," I simply ran with the evocative phrase, and my poem was the result.

Grin

Almost none of my oldest, deepest memories are more evocative or bewitching to me than my earliest memories of jack-o'-lanterns flickering in the dark on Halloween night.... No light flickered quite like jack-o'-lantern light, filtered as it was through the orange rinds of carven gourds, flashing as it did from the ink-black shadows that gather on porches after the lights have been turned off for the evening.... Add to all that the particular savory smell of pumpkin-flesh seared by candle-flame, and I am left with a primal impression printed on the very deepest corridor of my mind—the haunted corridor of childhood, which I am forever seeking, but to which I can never return.

The Stain

Again, this poem was directly based on a true story—with some fanciful embellishments. My mother was not happy....

The Candy Chute

During the Coronavirus Pandemic of 2020, Halloween enthusiasts developed an ingenious method for distributing candy—one that would pose no risk of spreading the deadly virus to trick-or-treating children. This was the Candy Chute—a usually colorful, decorated tube, of cardboard or PVC pipe, down which candy could be slid right into treat-buckets and bags. During this era of social distancing—of literal death and disease on an unfathomable scale unseen in modern times—this humble invention allowed for the hallowed rite of trick-or-treat to live on. Much to my extreme delight, on the night of Halloween 2020, I located a candy chute right around the corner from my house, and got to partake in its full treat-dispensing glory. It was literally the highlight of my evening—such a fun invention, even if borne out of grim necessity. This chute, as I remember it, had circus-like stripes, lights wrapped around its length, and emerged either through, or from beneath, the grimace of a ghostly mask—an apt metaphor for the invisible cloud of plague the candy chute sought to bridge.

The Halloween Owl

This poem was inspired by the goblinesque designs found on vintage die-cuts made by companies like Beistle. These cardboard cutouts usually featured a garish and uniquely distinctive color-palette of black, orange, green, and yellow.

In the Circle of Seven Jack-o'-Lanterns

This poem is loosely based on what I did one Halloween many years ago. I believe it was the first or second year I'd ever grown pumpkins, and in my exuberance, I had grown quite a few. Seven of them proved suitable for carving, so, the night before Halloween, in one fevered session (which resulted in quite a wicked case of neck pain), I carved seven jack-o'-lanterns. Having nothing much better to do on Halloween night, we arranged them in my garden, in a loose circle around my back porch area, and sat in the darkness watching them flicker, while sipping a special berry and wine concoction we had brewed up. In many ways, this arrangement was an art installation for me—an attempt bring some old-school Halloween atmosphere from my imagination into reality.

Autumn Witch

This poem is directly based off of an artwork by noted pinup artist Becca Whitaker, the original of which resides in my personal collection.

Loweena the Witch

The name Loweena is a simplification of Lloweenah, which itself is an anagram of Halloween. I came up with this name one afternoon while lying on my bed and staring at the stack of books on my nightstand. One of them was, of course, a book about Halloween, and as I stared at the title, the letters of the word Halloween rearranged themselves in my mind into the name Lloweenah. As for the literal backstory of this colorful character, not much is known... save that she once fell from the sky during a flying accident, and that her jack-o'-lantern broke her fall, branding her derriere with a coal-black pumpkin face.

The Scarecrow Maiden

This poem was directly inspired by a striking female scarecrow I saw while on a hayride one year at Tanaka Farms, in Irvine, California. It was an entry in a scarecrow competition, and I must say that it was the most bewitching scarecrow I have ever seen. It wore what appeared to be an old sort of wedding dress, and looked overall much like an archetypal harvest bride figure.

My October Bride

This poem is rife with actual details from my wedding—only woven into a weird, fantastical plot-line. Once again, this is a prime example of me simply describing real life, but then embellishing it further, with a story arising directly out of the imagery.

Dead Leaves

This poem was very nearly lost. Though I was dimly aware of its existence—having written it a number of years ago—it was somehow left out of my early drafts of this manuscript. While combing my old files for forgotten material, however, I was able to salvage it, and I'm quite pleased I did. I feel I captured—with rare poetic accuracy—the feeling that dead leaves evoke in me.

This Halloween

This poem is another fragment, a piece I had intended to be longer. I chose to include it anyway, as it seems to stand okay on its own.

Extinguished

This piece was an attempt to capture that familiar, fleeting melancholy I have experienced late at night on Halloweens past when I have blown out my jack-o'-lanterns for the evening. This act, more than any other, seems to signal the final conclusion of October's phantasmal festivities.

The Jack-o'-Lantern's Mark

This poem was actually inspired by my wife. She has been through a lot in life, and at times a certain sadness, mixed with the wisdom that follows, gathers around her like a shadow. In those times when I am facing something tough, and she is lending me the haunted lantern of her heart to show me the way through, I can see that she bears the Jack-o'-Lantern's Mark, the mark of a wayward soul.

One Last Little Jack-o'-Lantern

Yet another poem based on true events. It was late in November, and I had one little pumpkin left—grown myself—that was about to succumb to decay. Rather than let it waste away, I gave it an honorable death: it became a tiny jack-o'-lantern, grinning in the face of the eternal night that would soon claim it. For those who may not know, Martinmas, also known as Old Halloween, occurs on November 11th.

The Throne of Gourd and Bone

This poem is my reaction to the innumerable social media personalities who claim to essentially be the king or queen of Halloween. The so-called Halloween Lifestyle seems to be in vogue nowadays, and I can think of no other holiday where so many folks are seemingly competing to be its most extreme devotee. It seems to me, however, that many of these folks forget a central aspect of Halloween—Sacrifice. Giving away candy to intrepid children in the dark. Pouring your blood, sweat, and tears into the thirsty earth, in order to grow the pumpkins that will become your jack-o'-lanterns. Sparing no detail in erecting a truly haunted yard display for all to see. And, giving another year of your life in order to witness the glory of another Halloween. From ancient times, Sacrifice has always been a central theme of the Halloween season, whether the sacrifice of the farmers' long months of heat and toil, or the sacrifice of offerings to the powers of health and plenty. Halloween is not about getting, but giving. Halloween is not about the one, but the many. Halloween is not about You, or Me—it's so much greater, and it's much, much older.

Candy Sorting

This poem represents one of the most vivid and enduring Halloween memories I have. It was such a special time and atmosphere, those late-night moments after trick-or-treating, but before extinguishing the jack-o'-lanterns for bedtime. It was a liminal time, a phantasmal time, a time between time—a time when anything could happen. Spooks and spirits were real at this time—more real even than during trick-or-treating. I remember sitting on the soft, brown carpet, before the eerie glow of the TV, and how I would dump out my bag of candy, then sort it into little piles—the desirable and undesirable; the worst, the best, and the in between. It was as if I were sitting in the innermost sanctum of Halloween, at the heart of its Mysteries, after having partaken in all of its most sacred rites. It was an atmosphere pregnant with meaning and significance—though what it all meant, I was too young then to understand. The die-cuts of skull, witch, scarecrow, and ghost regarded me from the walls like silent hierophants of the ghoulish and grotesque. Only now, separated by the abyss of years, do I begin to piece together the deeper meaning of it all, and set it into words.

At Summer's Wistful End

I wrote this poem after I had conceived of the title for this book. It is simply another example of me basing a poem entirely on a title, and what it evoked in my imagination. This book's title was carefully conjured up over a series of afternoon walks, during which—by the ghostly golden light of summer evenings—I meditated on what this book was to be about, and what sort of sound, emotion and image I wanted the title to convey. It is intentionally shorter than the titles of the previous two entries, lending it a sort of sadness and finality fitting for the last volume in the series.

ABOUT THE CONTRIBUTORS

K. A. OPPERMAN is a poet and artist hailing from southern California. In addition to his Halloween poetry, Opperman is the author of two volumes of Gothic poetry: *The Crimson Tome* (2015) and *The Laughter of Ghouls* (2021), both published by Hippocampus Press. His work has appeared in *Midnight Under the Big Top* (Cemetery Dance Publications, 2020), *Black Wings of Cthulhu 6* (Titan Books, 2018), *Spectral Realms, Vastarien, Weirdbook, Weird Fiction Review, The Audient Void, Eye to the Telescope,* and many other venues.

DAN SAUER is a graphic designer and artist living in Oregon. In 2016, he co-founded (with editor/publisher Obadiah Baird) *The Audient Void: A Journal of Weird Fiction and Dark Fantasy,* which features his design and illustration work. Since 2017, he has worked extensively on book covers, interior art, and custom lettering for Hippocampus Press, Centipede Press, and other publishers. His art often takes the form of surreal collage and photomontage, as pioneered by artists such as Max Ernst, Wilfried Sätty, Harry O. Morris and J. K. Potter.

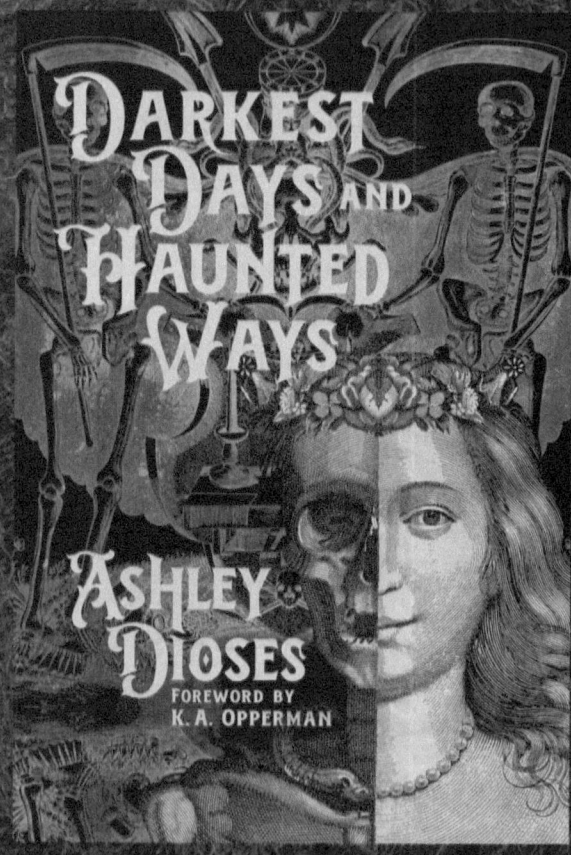

HALLOWEEN 💀 HEARTS

"Adele Gardner's **Halloween Hearts** presents a kaleidoscopic pageant of delightful October imagery. Haunted by the wistful ghost of childhood past, and paraded through by a midnight processional of witches and black cats, these pages provide a fine evening of autumnal entertainment."—**K. A. Opperman**, **author of *Past the Glad and Sunlit Season: Poems for Halloween***

Adele Gardner's *Halloween Hearts* is a welcome celebration of all things Halloween, whether they take place on October 31st or not. Disciples of All Hallows' Eve, enter of your own free will… haunted houses, trick-or-treaters, vampires, demonic foxes, witches and their familiars, revanants both longed-for and uninvited, and the creeping mists of autumn all have their place in these pages. Ray Bradbury and Edgar Allan Poe—icons of the American imagination, pilgrims of the nightside territories of the mind—have a special place in this book. In these poems, Gardner explores Poe's hallowed place in our haunted hearts, and lovingly celebrates Ray Bradbury and his unique alchemy of nostalgia, dread, and Halloween eternal.

". . . this book has been a long time coming, with its black cats and witches, ghosts and the grave, vampires and writers that haunt the night. Whether their subjects are traditional to Halloween or on tangential themes, all these poems are Halloween to me—that season so melancholy and elegiac, yet also fierce, with shining teeth, pointy grins, and a cat's fang-filled mischief." —**Adele Gardner**, from the introduction

AVAILABLE NOW FROM

JACKANAPES PRESS

www.JackanapesPress.com
www.facebook.com/Jackanapes-Press